The Gentle
On Datin

A Practical Guide on
How to Approach and Communicate
With Women

By K. Hicks

I gently touched her hand: she gave
A look that did my soul enslave;
I pressed her rebel lips in vain;
They rose up to be pressed again.
Thus happy. I no further meant,
Than to be pleased and innocent.

On her soft breast my hand I laid,
And a quick, light impression made;
They with a kindly warmth did glow,
And swelled, and seemed to overflow.
Yet, trust me, I no further meant,
Than to be pleased and innocent.

On her eyes my eyes did stay:
O'ver her smooth limbs my hands did stray;
Each sense was ravished with delight,
And my soul stood prepared for flight.
Blame me not if at last. I meant
More to be pleased than innocent.

Copyright Credits:
The author gratefully acknowledges permission excerpts from the following:

Ten Laws of Lasting Love, by Paul Pearsall, Ph.D., Copyright 1993, Simon & Schuster Inc.

You just don't understand: women and men in conversation, by Deborah Tannen, Ph.D. Copyright 1990, William Morrow and Company, Inc.

Love is never enough, by Aaron T. Beck, M.D., Copyright 1988, Harper & Row, Publishers, Inc.

How to make anyone fall in love with you, by Leil Lowndes, Copyright 1996, Contemporary Publishing.

Cracking the love code, by Janet O'Neal, Copyright 1998, Broadway Books, a division of Bantam Doubleday Dell Publishing Group, Inc.

Lee, J.A. "Love Styles," in R.J. Sternberg and M.L. Barnes, eds., The Psychology of Love. New Haven, CT, and London Yale Press, 1988.

Dover Publications, Inc.:
Old-Fashioned Love and Romance, Copyright 1989
1,001 Advertising Cuts from The Twenties and Thirties, Copyright 1987
1,337 Spot Illustrations of the Twenties and Thirties, Copyright 1992
Treasury of Art Nouveau Design & Ornaments, Copyright 1980

ISBN 0-9684498-0-8

Printed in Canada

CONTENTS

For love is strong as death, passion deep as the grave;
it blazes up like a blazing fire, fiercer than any flame.
Many waters can not quench love,
no flood can sweep it away.

There is a moon sole
in the blue night

amorous of waters
tremulous,
blinded with silence the
undulous heaven yearns where

in tense starlessness
anoint with ardor
the yellow lover

stands in the dumb dark
svelte and urgent

again love I slowly gather
of thy languorous mouth the
thrilling flower

as is the sea marvelous
from god's
hands which sent her forth
to sleep upon the world

and the earth withers
the moon crumbles
one by one
stars flutter into dust

but the sea
does not change
and she goes forth out of hands and
she returns into hands

and is with sleep…..

love,

the breaking
of your
soul
upon
my lips

Need Positive Change in your life ?
Remove stress / anxiety / reduce pain?
Call 416-562-2671 or e-mail to
Hypnosis_positivechange@rogers.com
Free Consultation

An Introduction:

Dating is an adventure, and just as you wouldn't go down the Amazon without a guide, you might want someone who knows the ins and outs of dating to show you the ropes. That's what this book is all about. Dating isn't scary, but it can be complicated, and that old Boy Scout advice might come in handy again: Be Prepared!

The main obstacle in developing a relationship today is getting past the initial barrier that separates a man and woman from freely connecting. This barrier is essentially a lack of communication and knowledge of how the opposite sex needs or likes to be approached and treated.

This book is designed to help men effectively appreciate and communicate on a woman's level of emotional intimacy. Hopefully, the "Gentleman's Black Book" will assist countless men in their quest of finding love and affection.

PART I
THE INITIAL APPROACH

A WOMAN'S NEEDS

1. Make her feel secure

For most of history, men have provided women with physical and financial security. In many ways men provided a means that was directly linked to a woman's physical survival thus making their women feel more secure.

Ah, for the simplicity of cavemen days. Things are different now. Today, most women make a living for themselves. The word "security" has taken on a significantly different meaning. Women no longer look to men as much for physical and financial security anymore; they look to them for emotional security. What emotional security really means to a woman is that she can count on her man. She needs to feel secure in his love.

Emotional security within a relationship involves several aspects:

Attractiveness:

It is especially important for a woman to know that the man in her life thinks that she is beautiful. Making her feel beautiful is not a one-time event, but an on-going process. Openly admire a woman and refrain from criticizing her. At the very least, make sure your criticism is constructive and loving.

Fidelity:

A woman needs to feel secure that her man is not going to stray. Although, he may look admiringly at other women, she needs to know that he will not act on anything. Take a cue from us. We have eyes too, but we know how to keep them in our heads.

Emotional Support:

If she has a bad day emotionally, she needs to know that he will be there to encourage her and really listen. A woman wants to be reassured of how important she is to her man. Sincere emotional support involves a degree of empathy and reassurance. Ultimately, self-esteem and security comes from within ourselves. But women continue to seek a sense of protection and security from men.

Caring:

When a man shows interest in a woman's feelings and heartfelt concern for her well-being, she feels loved and cared for. Naturally, she begins to trust him more. When she trusts, she becomes more open and receptive.

2. Make her your first priority

Making your woman a top priority doesn't mean that you have to sacrifice your interests and hobbies. Simply make your woman feel secure that she is the most important person in the world to you. Do this by prioritizing your relationship before your job, friends and outside activities. A secure woman will not put you in the difficult position of choosing between her and someone or something else held dear in your life (unless, of course, that thing happens to be womanizing.) She will simply have the confidence that you are there for her.

3. Pay attention to her

A woman needs her man's attention focused on her. As a healthy relationships progresses, a woman will feel that her happiness is a priority to her man. Paying attention to a woman goes deeper than simply noticing what is happening to her; it also involves loving support and acknowledgment. Remember it's a two-way road and you reap what you sow. Showing love and interest results in that love and interest being shown back to you.

When men focus their undivided attention on a woman during the stage of pursuit their stone-age manner simulates the male's primary activity of hunting. (Luckily most women don't have to worry about being dragged back to a cave by their hair anymore.) The man places his complete attention on her during that time because he is in active pursuit. So often, when he has "gotten" her, he doesn't feel he needs to pay attention anymore. Unfortunately, some men are better at getting what they want than keeping it.

4. Listening and Understanding

Men and women have different communication styles. They don't listen the same way. Problems due to these differences become more apparent when men and women are discussing their problems. Instead of offering solutions to your woman's problems, simply learn how to listen to her with your full attention. Show empathy towards her.

When a man listens without judgment but with empathy to a woman expressing her feelings, she feels heard and understood. An understanding attitude doesn't presume to already know a person's thoughts or feelings; instead it gathers meaning from what is heard, and moves toward validating what is being communicated. The more a woman feels she is being heard and understood, the more she will feel fulfilled, and the easier it is for her to give her man the acceptance he needs.

5. Romance and Affection

Show tender and loving forms of affection to your woman. Learn what makes her feel special. Buy her small personal gifts. (Don't scare her though. A two pound sapphire is not preferable to a little teddy bear.) Be generous to her with your affection.

6. Reassurance and Validation

A woman needs for her man to be truly supportive of her goals. Encourage her like you are her best friend. Partners who love and trust each other earn their healthy relationships by keeping up their ends of the emotional bargain. When a man does not object to or argue with a woman's feelings and wants but instead accepts and confirms their validity, a woman truly feels loved. A man's validating attitude confirms a woman's right to feel the way she does. (It is important to remember one can validate her point of view while having a different point of view.) Just remember there's an art to choosing your battles, though. It may not be important to prove to her that boxing

13

is an artform, not a barbaric display of male power.

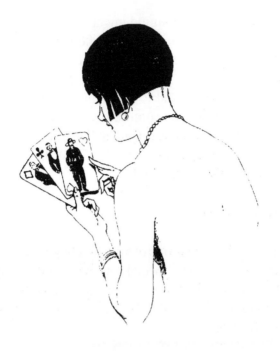

When one plays a game with a woman,
make sure she cannot see your cards.

You are the very one I've searched for
In many lands in every weather.
You are my sort; you understand me;
As equals we can talk together.

CONNECTING

1. Peace of mind and happiness depend on your state of mind -- not on your relationship or marital status.

Happiness, much like self-confidence comes from within. (So, unfortunately, does bad breath. But more on that later.) Enjoy life. It is healthy to set goals of finding a loving relationship. But it is also important to be happy during each stage of our life even when we are single. Experience your joy -- don't search for it.

2. Don't be too attached to the outcome of the relationship.

Make it your goal to attract people and connect with them, as opposed to attaching yourself to a specific result. This doesn't necessarily mean that you don't care about the relationship and the person you are involved with.

3. Two whole people make a relationship work, not two desperate people trying to fill up their own emptiness with someone else.

Connect with people who contribute positively in your life. Good relationships give you energy and ultimately enrich your being. Avoid emotionally unhealthy people. Unless you're writing a thesis or a novel about lunatics, leave them to their own devices.

You want a whole, vibrant and unique individual who has a full life. You want to be with someone who brings joy into a relationship, not someone who desperately looks to the relationship for their source of happiness.

4. Regardless of how attractive you are always be approachable. You have to get out and connect with people.

People don't generally connect with people who look unapproachable. If you rarely make eye contact, don't smile and you don't seem interested, you will have an extremely difficult time connecting with someone. If you appear too cool or aloof, people won't approach you. Remember, people are reading your face. Do you want it to say, "I'm full of painful existential angst"? Or would you like it to say, "I'm happy, confident, and probably a great conversationalist"?

5. People want to connect with confident, happy people.

People gravitate to smiling, happy and upbeat people. It is only natural to want to share in that person's joy. Project your own happiness and confidence. Concentrate on your personal strengths and what you take pride in. Build your confidence and think positive thoughts. "Smile and the world smiles with you." Develop your sense of humor and you will ultimately develop your sense of joy in life. Laughter is the greatest aphrodisiac in the world.

6. Show care and empathy.

We all need to feel that someone sincerely cares about us. The key to connection is talking about yourself and sharing you innermost feelings. How can I create a feeling of genuine caring? How? Find something about the woman's situation or personality to which you can relate. Perhaps you can remember a time when you felt a similar experience or emotion. Listen with your full attention.

Ask questions that show you're truly interested in what she thinks and feels.

7. Similarity - I am a lot like you, after all.

People like to be around other people who are like them. Find out something you and the woman have in common, and tell her. When you are talking with a new woman who expresses an interest in a topic that interests you let her know. By conversing on common ground with a new woman, you have established a measure of intimacy and therefore you both will feel more connected immediately. It is an attractive package to connect with someone who shares your interests; and who also contributes new ideas and experiences.

8. Look for one positive quality that you admire in a woman and share it with her. If you genuinely like someone, they usually like you back.

Be genuine when you compliment someone. Empty compliments appear manipulative. Direct your compliments to the woman's substance, rather than her physical appearance.

WHERE TO MEET NEW WOMEN

- Do something you enjoy.
- Choose places to go and things to do based on your personality style.
- Go to places where the type of mate you're looking for might be. E.g. If you like sporty women, frequent the athletic club or join sporting activities groups. If you like literary enthusiasts, attend poetry readings.

Always be ready. You could meet that special someone at the most unexpected times and places.

Research unique ways and places to meet someone:
- Yellow pages for groups and clubs.
- Neighborhood newspapers - check for special events and activities.
- Magazines for special interests and travel ideas
- Newspaper entertainment and arts section
- Cultural pamphlets and promotional information

Places to Meet New Women

Conferences and Trade Shows:
Wine and cheese, design and boat exhibitions. Make a point to attend shows that are specifically geared towards women. E.g.: fashion, cosmetic, cooking, and interior design exhibitions.

Cultural Events:
Museums, galleries, symphonies, galas and theatrical events.
Literary Events:
Festivals of authors, poetry readings and book signings
Festivals:
Oktoberfest, foreign film festivals, jazz festivals
Athletic Clubs:
Beach volleyball, tennis, skiing, cycling groups and wilderness tours
Social Clubs:
Sailing club, linguistic organizations
Hobby Clubs:
Horticultural associations and nature groups
Courses:
Karate, parachute, scuba diving lessons and air flight schools
Night School:
Cooking and foreign language classes
Performing Arts:
Dance studios, circus arts, acting lessons, creative writing workshops
Volunteering:
Charity work, wild life fund and human rights organizations
Networking:
Throw your own parties and invite your friends

Random places:
Blind dates, weddings, internet, book stores, political rallies, singles dances, pubs and stylish bistros

PUT YOUR BEST FOOT FORWARD

Dress to Kill:

Clothing drastically influences the perception a woman has of you. That perception is all they have to go on when they first meet you. Gentlemen, you don't have to wear a three piece suit everyday, but make an effort to look your best for all occasions. In every situation you have the potential to meet someone special. There is a wide variety of situations, E.g.: walking your dog, at the fruit stand or browsing through the magazine rack in the variety store. It's not necessary to put on a tuxedo to buy a pint of milk, (although if the urge strikes, who am I to quash it?) However, think of what it might cost you to walk down to the corner in flip-flops, your hair uncombed, in stained sweatpants? If the woman of your dreams walks by, she's more likely to toss you a nickel than she is to give you her phone number.

Generally, women are attracted to well-dressed, well-groomed successful looking men. Invest in an Italian suit, quality shoes and designer casual wear.

Keep yourself psychologically fit and open to opportunities of meeting new women. Remember, you only have one chance to make a first impression.

Walk with Confidence:

Looks are primarily more important to a man. But, various traits are equally or more important to a woman. E.g.: sense of humor, attentiveness and professional success.

We can't choose our looks but we can certainly enhance our appeal by good body language. Gentlemen, your physical movements undoubtedly affect how alluring you are to women. Dragging your knuckles along the ground is no longer considered an affective display of masculinity. Move in a strong, confident and masculine manner. Make bold, smooth, strong movements. Walk strong and look like a man who knows where he is going and why. When crossing the street, protectively take the lady's arm. Help her get in and out of a car. Exhibit masculine gestures which women find so alluring and seductive.

BODY PRAISE

When initially meeting a new lady, send off the right signals by showing her that you are interested. Physically express to her that she has captivated your attention and interest. Moderate your expressions so they are in keeping with the situation. So, instead of letting your tongue hang out, you might try one of the following:

Make eye contact:

Look directly into her eyes and maintain your deep gaze to create an emotional state. Make your own eyes warm and inviting. Prepare yourself for her to look away. Women have been conditioned to lower their eyes when men look at them. This doesn't necessarily mean that she is not interested. If she glances back at you within a few moments; she most probably welcomes your attention.

When you're chatting with a new lady, let your eyes linger on her a little longer - even during moments of silence. Move your gaze away slowly and reluctantly. Don't fake it, though. A smart woman will detect if you're acting like Rudolph Valentino. Be yourself, but be attentive.

Smile:

Make your smile exude warmth and friendliness.

Nod:

Should she glance back at you within a few moments, nod to her. Transfer a message of respectfulness.

Don't delay in approaching a woman that you would like to meet. Make your way towards her and move close enough to speak with her. Don't knock anyone over on your way to the bar (you don't want to look desperate). Make your approach casual so you put her at ease. Move and act in a relaxed fashion.

Initiate Conversation:

Don't use "opening lines". They sound insincere and extremely flat. Your first sentence could relate to the woman and/or the current situation. You could ask her how she knows the host/hostess of the party. Or compliment a particular piece of clothing or jewelry that she is wearing. Your first few sentences should be positive, happy and charming.

Here are a few that women would prefer never to hear again:
"Do you come here often?"
"Do I know you from somewhere?"
"Goodness, you're tall for a woman."
"I'll understand if you find me irresistible."

Try, for a change something like one of the following:
"You have a wonderful laugh."
"Have you tried the guacamole?"
Or why not simply say, "Hi. My name is _____," and
extend your hand. Being direct is not a bad thing.

Your opener doesn't necessarily have to be an intellectual
or profound statement. At this point she is checking you
out. During these first few moments, she is actively
assessing your overall aura and mannerism. When a
woman initially meets you she is making a subconscious
analysis of you as a potential partner. She is sampling you,
during those first few moments of your approach. Show
her what a wonderful partner you could be.

When the denial becomes fainter and fainter,
And her eyes give what her tongue deny
As what a trembling I feel when I venture,
Ah what a trembling does usher my Joy!

TECHNIQUES TO ESTABLISH INTIMACY

These proven techniques will undoubtedly aid you. But remember to be honest at all times. After all, you are dealing with a human being who has vulnerabilities and emotions.

Key Words:

If you detect any unusual words in her conversation, zero in on these words and initiate a conversation based on those topics. She may be referring to a subject which she would like to speak about. E.g. If she is commenting on the weather and uses the term "Windy City." Focus on these words and expand the conversation by talking about the city of Chicago.

Speak her Language:

Listen to the woman's unique choices of words which connects her to her own world of family and friends. Listen carefully, echo these words back to her to enhance closeness. Each woman uses a variety of words to describe places and things.

E.g. She may refer to her workplace, as the office or the firm. Use the same terminology.

When she refers to her nephew as a "little angel". Use the same expression, instead of child or baby. This will make her feel closer to you.

Similar Convictions:

Seek out a topic which is important to the woman, and listen to her opinions. If you have a similar conviction; share your ideas and beliefs. When you agree and understand about issues which are vital to her; this helps in drawing you together.

Body Language:

Once you have made the initial contact and you have greeted the lady, utilize effective body language to enhance intimacy.

Move your face receptively in her direction. Turn your shoulders, then your knees, until your bodies face each other. As you turn your body towards her, intimacy increases. Lean towards the lady to show that you are interested. Again, subtlety counts. If you look like you're tying yourself in a knot (or worse, like you're doing a slow-motion flamenco) you might be shooting yourself in the foot.

Touching:

When a man and woman meet each other, they may inadvertently touch each other. This type of touching is completely natural because they are not aware of their physical contact. When touching is given and received openly the effect can be intimately bonding.

A woman can easily become uncomfortable with physical contact from a man she doesn't know. She may interpret the touching as a sexual pass and therefore feel pressured. Avoid misunderstandings during the tender stages of romance. Give yourself time to get to know each other, to build trust and to ultimately bond.

* When in doubt - keep your hands to yourself.

First Conversation:

Attempt to make your first discussion flow smoothly.

Discover which conversational topic she finds exciting. E.g.: theater, foreign films, international travel.

Pay attention to her involuntary facial expressions and gestures. E.g.: eye fluctuation, head movements and hand gestures.

When her face sparks to life on a particular topic, continue conversing and asking questions on that subject.

If her expression grows bland that is your cue to curve the flow of the conversation in another direction. (Surprisingly, she just may not be interested in fluctuations in the stock market.)

When she finds the conversation stimulating she will keep her gaze focused on you. If her head starts to turn away switch to a new conversational subject. If her eyes close and her head nods forward, this is a signal that you may have put her to sleep. Try not to let things get this far.

If a woman is turning away call her by her name and ask her a personal question. This may recapture her attention. Occasionally, her eyes may wander; this is not necessarily a rejection of you. She could simply be bored with the topic of conversation. Change the conversational subject.

When someone is interested in a conversation their pupils grow larger; if disinterested their pupils start shrinking. Another good sign of a successful conversation is that you are not the only one leading it. If she's engaged, you won't have to try too hard to keep things going. Remember, if she's interested, she wants to keep you there, too.

Always speak with enthusiasm and confidence about your life. Don't concern yourself so much with using "great lines" when you meet a new woman. Elaborate on your conversation and share intriguing details. When asked a question, give additional information to help the flow of your dialogue. Add interesting diversity and flavor to your conversation. Overall, be yourself. No point in being someone else for the first half hour, and then finally having to show who you really are. Being natural is a natural turn on. So don't fake it, fellas.

Levels of Conversation:

Level One: Clichés
Strangers speak using clichés. They chat about safe topics, E.g.: weather. "Well, it certainly is blustery today, wouldn't you say?"

Level Two: Facts
Acquaintances discuss facts. "The Blue Jays are on quite a tear."

Level Three: Feelings and Personal Questions
Friends express their feelings to each other. They ask personal opinions and questions. "Do you like this shirt on me?"

Level Four: "We" Statements

Close friends and lovers use this level of conversation of intimacy. It goes beyond clichés, facts and reaches a deeper level than feelings.

To create a sense of intimacy with a new woman, speak with her using the higher levels of conversation. Ask her her feelings on something, similar to the manner you would ask a close friend. Use the term "we" to create a closer connection.

E.g.: Personal Question: Do you enjoy dancing under the stars?
E.g.: "We" Statements: We are going to have a good time tonight.

Foibles:

If your conversation is flowing smoothly with a new woman you could give a minute "foible" about yourself. Make sure that the "foible" (mistake) is very minor. E.g.: "I have a sweet tooth, I'm sure you can tell," instead of, "I have a nasty habit of stealing cars once in a while." This type of confession can create intimacy.

Show her that you are the man she has been waiting for:

Find out what qualities she admires. Show the lady how skilled you are in what she regards as redeeming virtues.

Each woman likes to be perceived in a different way. Read between the lines to uncover how she sees herself. Nurture her self image with your support.

1. Show her that she has captivated you by her charm.
2. Reveal your compassion.
3. Vocalize your approval and admiration.
4. Bestow on her your genuine praise and compliments.

Empathy and Compassion:

Let her know how much you agree and understand how she feels. Call her by her name frequently.

Show your support: E.g.: I understand how you must have felt.
E.g.: I would have done the same thing.

Use the proper body language to send a message of understanding and empathy. Open body language -- arms uncrossed, face forward -- is more inviting than someone who is clenched into a ball in their seat.

Take note of the concerns in her life. Make references to the tiniest details of her life. You will make her feel special.

Share a Private Joke:

To create early intimacy, listen to her story and choose a phrase that she delights in. Repeat back to her that favorite phrase. You can share a small joke, like long time lovers. Only choose the part of the story where she shines. She will warm to your attentiveness.

Words of Endearment

Admiration:

Women respond receptively to expressions of admiration, especially for their accomplishments. As the conversation flows add your notes of approval. (Not full blown compliments) E.g.: That's impressive. You have wonderful insight.

Implied Compliment:

Indirectly praise her, in the early stage of romantic development. Imply that she is wonderful. Do not appear to be intentionally complementing her. E.g.: I am sure that you're not old enough to remember this..... Anyone as good looking as you.... Exceptionally creative people like you.....
Saying, "Gracious, you'd make a good mother" might be a bit much at this stage.

I like what you like about yourself:

Discover what the lady takes personal pride in. Carefully listen to her and find out her passions. She will be so much more responsive when you compliment her on a prized accomplishment. Determine what she would like you to recognize her for. Does she consider herself E.g.: creative? stylish? intellectual?

Extremely attractive women prefer to be complemented on their talents rather than their physical appearance.

She will be even more receptive to you when you praise a recent accomplishment.

Knock Out Compliment:

Initially use words of empathy, approval and praise. Save up your knock out compliment. A knock out compliment is designed to take a woman's breath away. But it's risky, too. You can't take back a knock-out compliment, so be careful when you choose to use one. As a rule, it's not such a good idea on a first date.

Avoid giving obvious compliments. Search for an original quality about a woman, one so deep that most people won't comment on it. Look her directly in the eyes, using her name, deliver the "knock out" compliment. Deliver your compliment in one strong, sharp sentence. "Knock out" compliments are even more effective when you are parting -- you'll leave her speechless.

Be sure to comment on something that she is proud of. Shoot the compliment high enough. When in doubt, aim even higher.

34

Ideas for good knock-out compliments:
"I figured out why you're single. Someone up there likes me."
"It's been hard walking all night with my knees weak."
"I'd love to take you to the art gallery, but I'm worried someone will try to put a frame around you."

Not so good ideas for knock-out compliments:
"I like you so much, I think I'll follow you everywhere you go."
"If I were a woman, I'd like to look like you."
"I'm not worthy of you, oh goddess."

Enjoy her compliments:

When a woman compliments you, receive the compliment graciously and transmit the same positive feelings back to her. Smile and thank her for noticing. Try not to fall into a dead faint.

Tell her that you care:

Tell your lady what you appreciate about her. So she will continue doing the things that you love. People fall in love for a multitude of reasons. You may have fallen in love with her affectionate nature and the way she caresses your hair. Encourage what you admire and tell her how much her affection means to you.

Communication is:
How to talk so others will listen;
How to listen so others will talk;
How to understand so love can win.

Without honesty there is no truth;
Without truth there is no understanding;
Without understanding there is no love;
Without love there is nothing.

COMMUNICATION - GENDER MENDER

Gender Problem Solving:

Differences in communication styles between the sexes are perhaps more apparent when, it comes to problem solving. When a problem comes up, there are three basic steps in discussing it: the problem, the feelings about it, and the solution.

Men tend to skip step two, while women tend to dwell on step two. Women like talking about problems; it makes them feel better to express their feelings about things even if they don't reach a solution. Men, on the other hand, feel frustrated until they do something to solve the problem.

Men and women are raised with different expectations and communication styles.

EMOTIONAL INTELLIGENCE
THE LANGUAGE OF INTIMACY

Ask an emotionally based question:

When a woman is conversing, you should interject by asking emotionally based questions. Women are in touch with their feelings; and they usually like discussing how they feel.

Speak words of sensitivity:

When speaking with a woman, intelligently discuss sensitive subjects which will interest her. At all times look, walk and act like a man. Speak with a deep voice. Being an intriguing conversationalist will not take away from your masculinity. It will only add an intriguing multidimensional feature to your characteristics. A woman will appreciate your understanding and relate better to you.

Discover her philosophical language:

Men and women enjoy speaking about different topics. Learn how to captivate women with your conversation. Explore the topics that interest her. Women enjoy discussing the arts, personal growth, health and spiritual subjects. Gear your conversations to a more psychological content. Converse with women in terms of feelings, philosophy, intuition and people. Openly discuss insights into people and their feelings.

Read between the lines:

Instead of telling a woman what the two of you are going to do -- ask her opinion first. When a woman asks a question don't always take it literally. Read between the lines; she may be hinting about something. If she asks "Would you like to," it most likely means she would like to.

Go to her assistance:

When you see a woman struggling with something, go to her and ask if she needs assistance. Unlike your male friends, she will not presume that you don't trust her capabilities. She will simply interpret your help as caring about her and her problems.

Say you're sorry:

Gentlemen, when you make a mistake, have the courage to say "I'm sorry." Women don't hear "I'm sorry" from a man very often.

If you do not know - just ask:

Gentlemen, if you need to know something - just ask. Seeking instruction and information is not necessarily a character weakness.

Know when to listen:

How to deal with a woman who looks upset or annoyed? Ask her if she wants to talk about it. Let her know that you are there for her. Ask her to share her feelings with you. Persist gently. Listen to her patiently. By listening you will help her get whatever is bothering her out of her system. Once she has communicated her distress you could possibly offer gentle answers. Do not feel that it is your responsibility to solve her problems. Just listen. She will see you as a more loving man.

The meeting of two personalities is like the contact of two chemical substances; if there is any reaction, both are transformed.

To laugh is to risk appearing the fool.
To weep is to risk appearing sentimental.
To reach out is to risk involvement.
To expose feelings is to risk exposing
your true self.
To place your ideas and dreams before the crowd
is to risk their love.
To love is to risk not being loved in return.
To live is to risk dying.
To hope is to risk despair.
To try is to risk failure.
But the greatest hazard in life is to risk nothing.
The one who risks nothing does nothing
and has nothing -
and finally is nothing.
He may avoid sufferings and sorrow,
But he simply cannot learn, feel,
change, grow or love.
Chained by his certitude, he is a slave, he has
forfeited freedom.
Only one who risks is free!

PART II

MAKING CONTACT

DATING

When to ask her out on a date:

How soon after meeting a new lady should you ask her out on a date? As a general rule, it is best to wait until she's finished telling you her name. Seriously, though, you should use your judgment. Asking someone out is a general assumption of interest on both parts. Let her feel that she has earned your interest or attentions through her charm, intelligence and unique personality.

Before a woman invests in an evening with you, she wants to know that she is going to enjoy herself and be secure. Give her enough information, so she can make a decision. Woman consider a wide range of aspects before going out with a man. E.g.: personality, intelligence and sense of humor. If you ask her out too soon, she may assume that you are only interested in her looks. A woman will value your interest in her if she feels that you appreciate her other qualities.

Dating - The Smooth Steps to Romance:

I conducted a romance survey with various women. One of my survey's questions related to where a woman would like to go on a first date with a new man.

I gave four choices:

      Big budget theatrical event
      Dinner in an elegant restaurant
      Coffee and dessert in a quaint cafe
      Walk in the park or along the boardwalk.

To my surprise, every women I surveyed chose a walk in the park or along the boardwalk. After thinking about it, it occurred to me that it was a perfectly reasonable choice for a woman to make. Atmosphere is extremely important to women; generally they are more esthetically inclined. After all, what could be more romantically moving on a date; than to be surrounded by natural beauty?

When asking the lady out:

Make the invitation casual. Invite the lady to join you for a coffee and dessert. You could casually invite her out for a pizza. On the first date, plan an activity that doesn't require that you spend the entire evening with the person. If the date is not going particularly well you can make a polite early departure.

Atmosphere, Atmosphere, Atmosphere:

Take your date to a restaurant that has charm and is relatively inexpensive. Decide on a place that has the atmosphere you would like to project, E.g.: creative, sophisticated, stylish. Atmosphere is especially significant to women. She will transfer her feelings about the room to you. Choose a bistro with a window view of a lake or a forest. Select a patio setting that overlooks a scenic ravine. An appealing view will give you both something beautiful and interesting to admire while you are getting to know each other. Conversely, a table beside the bathrooms might have an unwanted effect. Select a place where you have enough privacy to talk freely.

Keep it simple:

Keep the first date simple and somewhat predictable. Plan a pleasant time to get to know each other a little better. Don't do anything that adds to the inherent discomfort of a first date. Bad ideas for first dates might be such things as bringing your date to a family reunion, or taking a long walk in a bad part of town. The purpose of the first date is to confirm an initial attraction. At this early stage, you just want to spend some time getting to know one another. A first date is not a stage for you to try to impress your date.

Plan ahead:

You should definitely have a good idea of where you would like to take the lady. But don't plan an evening so tightly that you preclude any spontaneity, since she may have an idea of her own. Be willing to forfeit your plans if she makes a reasonable alternative.

Make sure you know the exact directions of where you are going. If you are not sure call in advance. Also inquire about parking space and menu costs. Avoid unexpected surprises. It's not nice to spend your special time together plotting coordinates in the middle of nowhere.

Assure mutual comfort:

Choose a location you are familiar with and where you will feel somewhat in control. Show your date how at ease you are. Your assured comfort will help her feel more relaxed.

A glass of wine or a beer can definitely help relax you. But it is preferable to abstain so you can keep your instincts alert. If you can't abstain, know your limits. Most women prefer their men (at least on first dates) sober and alert. Falling off your chair while singing "Feelings" is a definite no-no. Remember that at this point you are trying to determine if you and this lady have potential. Alcohol can alter your personality and it is important that you both see each other for who you really are.

Behave like a gentleman:

Always open the door for the lady. Gently help her on with her coat. Graciously take her arm when crossing the street. Adapt a gentleman-like attitude of consideration for a woman's comfort on a date. Be attentive to her desire and needs. Be sensitive to her physical comfort — is she chilly? Be considerate, but not fawning. Again, stay natural. (If she wanted a butler, she'd hire one.)

Pay attention to her desires:

Pay close attention to your date's wishes. Make personal suggestions from the menu — ask her what her favorite cuisine is. Inquire if she needs something from the waiter. Would you like another cappuccino? Show her that you want to care for her. Let her know that you are looking out for her. After she finishes her meal, encourage her to have dessert or a specialty coffee. Show her that you want to be generous with her.

Admire her:

Give her admiring glances and praise. Subtly compliment her outfit. Women spend a considerable amount of time preparing themselves to look good on a date. Your new lady friend especially wants to look good for you.

Ask her questions:

Ask her where she was raised. Ask her about her studies and why she choose her career. Ask about her interests and about her future ambitions.

Listen attentively to everything she says. Show her how important her company is to you. Make your questions somewhat personal, but don't attempt to plunge too deeply into her private life. Avoid asking prying questions. (It might be too early to inquire what side of the bed she likes to sleep on, for instance.) Remember, it takes time to get to know someone. Find out her interests and about some of her enjoyable life experiences. At this point, you are testing the waters and becoming more acquainted. If you stumble onto a difficult subject; change the topic. Attempt to make the conversation as smooth as possible.

Be optimistic at all times especially concerning your future. If you are not yet professionally established, talk to her about the positive plans you have for the future.

Focus on her:

Make her the primary focus. Woman love to have your undivided attention. Treat her like she is the most beautiful woman in the room. Refrain from looking at other woman. (You can look at the waitress. Briefly.) Show her how important her company is to you.

At the end of the date:

Be very polite to the server and tip well. An attentive date always watches how you treat other people.

When you drive the lady home, attempt to confirm your next date. Casually mention that there is a good movie playing on the weekend. Invite her out to an interesting Asian restaurant. If she responds to your invitation evasively tell her that you will call her later in the week to confirm plans.

A hand shake or a quick kiss on the cheek is fine. Don't push to establish a sexual relationship too quickly. If she expects anything more, she'll let you know. Take your time and get to know her. Avoid any misunderstandings that could hinder your relationship.

A ROMANTIC ASSESSMENT

After the date ask yourself:
- Do you have anything in common with her?
- Was she unresponsive or distant at times?
- Was her attention towards you inconsistent?
- Did you have a good time?
- Did she seem to enjoy your company?

After some time, reflect and ask yourself:
- Does she neglect to return your calls?
- Has she turned down two or more of your invitations?
- Has she turned down ten or more of your invitations?
(This might be a sign to give up and turn your attentions elsewhere.)

By the second date, you're getting to know each other a little better. Spend your time together having fun while you go through the stages of connecting. You'll be learning more about the person, but that should come in the natural flow of things. Don't force it. Don't pry. Intimacy is a process that develops; it is impossible to establish instant intimacy.

By the third date you're probably making a decision on how much you want to invest in the relationship. Also, by the second and third dates, you should be able to detect the signs of any critical flaws in a person.

Key to Compatibility is:
Acceptance, Appreciation, Adjustment

How Compatible are you:
- Do the two of you have similar values?
- Can you resolve your differences?
- Do you have similar needs for closeness or separateness?
- Do you have similar lifestyles and goals?

Avoid a person with critical flaws such as:

Addiction
Anger or rage
Emotionally unavailability
Obsessive types
Insecure or paranoid types
Non-commitment problem
Narcissism or self-centeredness
Immaturity or irresponsibility

Everyone of us has a degree of imperfection in their personality. How much we should tolerate will depend on what is acceptable or unacceptable to each individual.

The soul attracts what it secretly harbors.

A ROMANTIC GUIDELINE

Your goal is to get past the first three dates. Give yourself a chance. Don't turn her off — before you even have a chance to get to know each other.

Date don'ts:

Don't give any detrimental information concerning your past. She will learn more about you as time goes by. Put your best foot forward. Be genuine — but always show her the best aspects of your character. She is actively looking, listening and waiting to discover every aspect about you.

Don't draw attention to a personal flaw. It may shock her to learn that you are under six foot, for example. She might not notice a physical or personality imperfection so much if you had not pointed it out to her. After all, no one is perfect.

Don't talk about marriage and the desire to have children. These are serious topics. At this early stage, you are both just getting to know each other. The courtship period should be fun and exciting. Once you have established that you like each other talk about these important issues. Make sure that she has the same plans and expectations for the future.

Don't jump into a sexual relationship too soon. Take time to get to know each other. Attempt to build a strong solid foundation of trust and understanding before you hurry into a physical relationship. (Remember once you start kissing, you can't go back to holding hands.)

Don't talk about ex-girlfriends. Don't relay a message that you still have feelings for a woman in your past. Don't talk about women in your past who have left you. It's also considered poor manners to actually bring ex-girlfriends along on dates. (We know you wouldn't...but a corollary of this is making sure the right name is coming out of your mouth at all times.)

Don't ask your date to talk about her ex-boyfriends. You may be stirring up some painful memories. If she wants to talk about a man in her past listen attentively, then attempt to move on.

Don't initiate conversations about sex. Remember she is on guard -- she is unsure of your intentions.

Don't seek reassurance from a woman, at least initially. It is a turn off when a woman senses fear and insecurity in a man. Remember, women look to men for security. Wait until you have established a relationship before opening up and sharing your concerns. Crying on a first date is especially frowned upon.

Don't monopolize the conversation. Avoid coming across as being self absorbed.

Don't give a woman your card and say, "call me." This puts the woman in an uncomfortable situation. It is inappropriate to expect her to be the one to call.

WORDS OF WISDOM

We're not so different after all:

Don't make a wide distinction between men and women. There are so many types of people; and there are so many different types of men and women. Approach a woman as an individual. We all have our own pattern of speech and communication, and these patterns often have less to do with sexual and gender stereotypes than with childhood values and experiences.

Know when to stay quiet:

Do not criticize a woman's physical appearance. Never give your personal opinion of her figure. Simply tell her she looks wonderful. Intentional or unintentional criticism of a woman's appearance is extremely detrimental to the well-being of the relationship.

Play the numbers game:

Approach as many women as your lifestyle permits. Always be actively looking. Don't take rejection too personally. Women have varied tastes and each one of us seeks diversified qualities. If a woman doesn't respond to your attentions it isn't necessarily a rejection of you. Move on; approach the next lady and the one after her. Play the numbers game and your chances of meeting someone will increase significantly.

It's still your move:

Despite changing roles and women's liberalization; it is still the man's responsibility to make the initial move and to actively pursue the woman. There are exceptions to this, but sadly, the ball's really in your court at the beginning. You have a definite advantage, make good use of it. Woman are held back by social restraints. Times are changing, but not as rapidly as you may think.

Women enjoy attention from men; they find it flattering. They want to be approached. Women spend an enormous amount of time, money and energy to look attractive for men. If you notice an unaccompanied woman in a single's social setting, she most probably came out hoping to meet someone new. Go ahead and approach her; she will be glad that you noticed her.

Enhance your chances:

Undoubtedly, the most attractive woman in the room will capture your attention. But, attempt to focus your attention on women who are on the same level of physical attractiveness as yourself. Set realistic expectations and increase your chances of success by pursuing women who are as equally attractive as yourself. Keep in mind that the Princess of Monaco is spoken for. (This week.)

GREAT PLACES TO TAKE YOUR DATE

Find out what your date's interests are. Plan an activity based on her interests. She will appreciate your thoughtfulness. An interesting activity takes the pressure off slightly, by adding an opportunity for conversation and fun.

If she likes the outdoors: Invite her for an afternoon barbecue beside the lake. Bring along your bikes to cycle around the park grounds. Or take her out for a picnic lunch in the park. Prepare a gourmet lunch basket. Bring along a large blanket to lie on and a few good books. Go for a walk through a dense forest. Feed the ducks.

History buff: Take her on heritage walking tour. Share her interest of yesteryear.

Eclectic type: Take her for a ride in the country and visit an antique show and interesting flea market.

Theater lover: Invite her to see an off-Broadway play. If she truly appreciates live drama — she will enjoy various aspects of the production. Choose a light comedy plot.

Science or archeology lover: Take her to the science center or go explore the dinosaur collection at the museum.

Animal lover: Invite her to the zoo. Have fun admiring the animal kingdom.

Literary enthusiast: Invite her to a poetry reading.

Be creative and innovative when planning activities for a date. Invite her to see a foreign film. Take her to the all-you-can-eat Chinese buffet dinner.

* Plan day trips initially. Thoroughly research the activities to know the directions, costs, hours of operation and where to park. Avoid unexpected surprises.

DANGER DATE - A NATURAL APHRODISIAC

There is impressive evidence and research which reveals that your newly acquainted lady will be more attracted to you if you place her in an emotionally stirring or very slightly dangerous situation. There is a strong link between emotional arousal and sexual attraction. Experimentation concludes that fear-producing situations can create a more erotic arousal.

To induce such an effect take your date horseback riding, to a frightening film, or a moving musical opera. Don't try to scare her intentionally, like taking her bungy jumping. Neither should you do anything too dangerous. The idea of a first date is that a second one should be possible. This is hard to guarantee if your first date is spent shooting the rapids.

MONEY MATTERS

Thanks to my romance survey, I was able to determine one important element. Men do not have to spend a lot of money on dating. Women prefer a walk in the park or along the boardwalk with a new man. Their second choice was a coffee and cake in a quaint cafe. Neither of these dating suggestions require much money.

I strongly discourage men from spending large amounts of money on their dates. Why spend your hard-earned money on a woman you may never see again? After a few dates you may realize that you have nothing in common. Women can occasionally feel uncomfortable or even obligated when a man (stranger) spends a sizable amount of money on them. Wait to get to know her and in the meantime, shower her with your attention.

Frequently women go out with men simply for companionship. Of course, there is nothing wrong with just being friends. Attempt to discover if this is the case, to avoid disappointments. Be subtle at all times. There are also those (rare) types of woman who are exclusively interested in what you have to offer them. Carefully conceal your "pocket book" from these ladies and they will quickly flee.

Do not talk about your personal financial affairs with a new woman. Do not discuss the topic of money at any length. Do not complain about your salary, do not talk about your investment losses and don't ask her how much money she makes. Money should not be an issue in the first stages of your relationship. Spend your energy (not your money) getting to know her.

If you have a restricted budget, organize cost efficient dates. E.g.: cook dinner for her, go to a movie, tour the local museums. Don't be cheap, though. Watching parking meters expire is only of interest to a very small minority of people.

Don't expect or ask your date to pay her way. Even if she offers — refuse to take her money. The worst turn off for a woman is when a man does not want to treat her. Wait until you and the lady have established a relationship - before considering splitting the bill.

When a man treats a woman to dinner she interprets it as an act of caring. The amount of money he spends is not so important as his gesture to treat her. This is related to her need of nurturing and security.

The minute you walked in the joint,
I could see you were a man of distinction,
A real big spender.
Good looking, so refined,
Say, wouldn't you like to know what's going on in my mind?
So let me get right to the point.
I don't pop my cork for every guy I see.
Hey! Big spender, spend a little time with me.

Love's not Time's fool, though rosy lips and cheeks
Within his bending sickle's compass come.
Love alters not with his brief hours and weeks,
But bears it out even to the edge of doom.

The lithe, handsome youth ran swiftly over
the fields to the dwelling of his beloved.
He knocked vigorously, and to her question,
"Who is it?" cried "It is thy lover!"
The door remained barred.
Crestfallen, he withdrew to meditate.

Hours later at evening he returned, this time
to tap gently at the door. When her question
came again, "Who is it?" he whispered
"It is thyself!" and was immediately
admitted to her embrace.

Arabian Legend

GOOD APPROACHES

I asked various women to give suggestions on how men could approach and initiate conversations with women. After pondering on the question, each lady agreed that it is undoubtedly a difficult task for men. All of the women I questioned simply encouraged men to be themselves.

Informative approach:

Men have been conditioned psychologically to be givers of information. Women traditionally have been given the role of receivers of information. Women will respect you for giving interesting and useful information. Women have always admired knowledge and intelligence in a man.

If your approach is subtle enough, she may not even be aware that you are "making a pass." In a way you are not "making a pass," you are simply getting to know each other — in the most natural sense.

Casual Approaches:

Act as natural as possible; unassuming and casual approaches go a long way. Talk to her like a friend. Gear your conversation to general subjects, this will take the pressure off you and the woman. E.g.: if you meet each other in the park, talk about the recreational activities which are offered. E.g.: talk to her about the outdoor Olympic swimming pool or the volley ball court. Talk about athletic activities that you enjoy. Ask questions. Invite her to join you in an activity. E.g.: swimming, baseball or a volleyball game. Smile and be friendly.

A good style of initiating conversation is an informative, nonthreatening discussion. E.g.: If a man was standing near a couple of attractive women in a stylish bistro, the man could initiate a conversation by passing on information. He could talk about the decor, (which is an interesting topic for women). The man could pass on unusual information concerning the rare antiquities in the bistro. He could elaborate his conversation by sharing interesting details of their time eras.

Conversations can also be initiated by passing on tidbits of information concerning new restaurants and lounges. Give interesting details about the atmosphere, type of crowd, and make suggestions of desirable entreés on the menu.

Casual informative conversations can be extended, when the man asks subtle questions. Keep in mind, some women don't like talking about their personal life or work. So make your questions general.

Use the informative approach in a wide range of scenarios.

If a man was ice-skating at the city hall, and he noticed a woman that he would like to approach, he could initiate a conversation by talking about the city hall.

Example: "Hello. It certainly is a great night for skating. It was a wonderful idea to have a skating rink designed in front of the city hall. Actually, the city hall itself is quite a unique building; it was constructed in 1965. They had an international contest, in which various architects from all over the world, submitted their designs. If you look closely you will see that the building is styled in the shape of two hands which enclose a round globe. This design symbolizes the strong multi-cultural aspect of Toronto."

Each approach depends on the situation. If a man frequented the ice rink regularly and noticed a familiar female face; he could make his approach gradual. He could initially say hello, another time he could strike up a short conversation about the rink. The man could position himself near her during intermissions. Eventually, he could ask her out for a coffee. It's not recommended that you actually skate into someone who interests you. That's literally getting things off on the wrong foot. However, a well-timed fall might give you the opening you're looking for!

COFFEE, TEA OR ME?

Invite her for a coffee:

Do not let an extended period of time pass before approaching a woman. As time goes by it could become even more difficult to approach her. As a rule, waiting so long that she leaves the building is not a positive approach. She may give up waiting for you to ask her out; and meet someone else in the meantime.

In almost any situation, it is perfectly acceptable to invite a woman to join you for a coffee. It is preferable that the cafe is within a few minutes walking distance. Make the invitation non-threatening and sociable. Most woman will be at ease, having a casual coffee with a new man. If she refuses your offer she is probably not interested. Don't waste your time pursuing someone who is not interested -- move on.

Break the ice:

If you were interested in a woman who worked in a store, near your home or workplace. You could approach her by making small talk, smiling and being friendly. You could mention that you are going for a coffee. Ask her if she wants anything. If she refuses, go ahead any way and bring her a specialty coffee. Smile, quickly put the cappuccino on the counter and leave. She will most probably say "You shouldn't have." But, she will undoubtedly appreciate the gesture and think well of you. This is an act of friendship and a good way to break the ice. Assume that if the coffee didn't work you should probably move on. At this point bringing her a smoked salmon probably won't work either.

*Love, what is it? "Tis very much like light, a thing that everybody
knows, and yet none can tell what to make of it. Tis not money,
fortune, jointure, raving, stabbling, hanging, romancing,
flouncing, swearing, ramping, desiring, fighting, dicing, though
all those have been, are, and still will be mistaken and miscalled
for it….Tis extremely like a sign, and could we find a painter
who could draw one, you'd easily mistake it for the other.*

PART III

AN EDUCATED LOOK AT RELATIONSHIPS

Three Modes of Attraction:

There are three ways in which men and women may be attracted to each other:

1. Visual: Being attracted to the way someone looks.

2. Auditory: Being turned on by a person's voice and what the person says — compliments, encouragement, etc.

3. Kinesthetic: Being warmed or turned on by someone's touch.

Three Types of Attraction:

1. Intellectual: You are mentally intrigued and challenged by the other person. You share and exchange ideas with each other.

2. Emotional: You feel safe enough with this person to share your most intimate thoughts. You can talk about your past, your future dreams, and even your deepest fear, knowing your trust will not be betrayed in any way.

3. Physical: Chemistry is derived from a unique physical and psychological response. It is an emotional current that flows between men and women.

In an article entitled "The Styles of Loving," John Alan Lee labels the Six Types of Love:

Erotic lovers get taken with each other very quickly, they establish physical intimacy almost immediately. They are demanding of physical perfection. Erotic lovers are principally concerned with beauty; personal and intellectual qualities come second. Once a suitable partner is found, there is a strong desire for intimacy. However, erotic lovers are not needy, possessive, or afraid to be alone; rather, they tend to be self-assured types who are willing to pursue an ideal.

Ludic lovers are playful types for whom love is a pastime. They do not get deeply involved emotionally, and don't want their partners too involved with them either. Often they date several people at the same time, and take care not to see anyone too often.

Storgic Love develops slowly, quietly and without great passion. It is more friendly and tends to grow between people who live or work near each other, between whom an increasing fondness grows over time. Intimacy develops later in the relationship. Usually their goals involve marriage and children.

Manic lovers get consumed by thoughts of the other, experience incredible highs when things go well, and sink to the depth of despair if the partner seems not to be responding fully. Manic love is like an emotional roller coaster. It is the stuff of romantic literature, full of passion, jealousy, and possessiveness.

Pragma love is known as "love with a shopping list". These lovers choose each other to be compatible in their interests, background and personalities. Intense feelings can develop with time, but the primary consideration is a practical match. Many arranged marriages are of this type.

Agape love demands total compassion, altruism and nondemandingness in their love. It involves a spiritual connection between a man and a woman.

THE PHYSICAL SIDE OF FALLING IN LOVE

Falling in love is both a mental and physical process. Scientists tell us that PEA-brained people fall in love. At the core of infatuation, they speculate, is a chemical called phenylethylamine, or PEA. It is a chemical cousin of amphetamines and gives a similar "kick."

PEA comes from secretions through the nervous system and bloodstream that create an emotional response equivalent to a high on drugs. This is the chemical which makes your heart palpitate and your hands sweat.

Phenylethylamine, scientists say, along with dopamine and norepinephrine, is manufactured in the body when we first feel the physical sensations of romantic love. It is as close to a natural high as the body can get.

Normally, the PEA high is too stressful to be sustained continuously without damage. Healthy long-lasting attachment love, on the other hand, is associated with the production of endorphins (morphine-like neurotransmitters), which yield a calmer, steadier, good feeling.

Although, neurotransmitters may provide the motive power for different kinds of love, they do not determine specific ways of feelings and behaviour. We often learn how to love from the society around us and from our own experiences.

Why do we Fall in Love with One Person and Not Another?

People don't just mysteriously wake up one morning with an overdose of PEA in their brains and then develop a crush on the next person they set eyes on. No, PEA, and its sister chemicals are precipitated by emotional and visceral reactions to a specific stimulus. Like what? It could be a whiff of her perfume or the adorable way she giggles. It could be the way she tosses her long hair away from her face or the youthful skip in her walk.

How Can These Little Things Start Love?

Why do these seemingly meaningless stimuli kick-start love? Where do they come from? No, genes have nothing to do with falling in love. The origin lies deeply buried in our psyche. The ammunition that gets fired off when we see (hear, smell, feel) something we like is lying dormant in our subconscious. It springs from that apparently bottomless well from which most of our personality rises -- our childhood experiences. When we are very young, a type of subconscious imprinting takes place.

A respected sexologist named, Dr. John Money defined the term Lovemap to describe this imprinting. Our Lovemaps are etchings of pain or pleasure axed in our brains in early responses to our family members or childhood friends. These imprints are so deep that they fester forever in some nook or cranny of the human psyche, just waiting for the appropriate stimuli to strike.

Dr. Money indicates that "Lovemaps are as common as faces, bodies and brains. Each of us has one. Without it there would be no falling in love, no mating, and no

69

breeding of species." We all have our own lovemap which is etched into our egos, our ids, our psyches, and our subconscious.

There are many theories about how and why we choose our love partner. But clearly, there is still a large element of mystery involved.

Paul Pearsall, P.h.D., in his book, "Ten laws of lasting love", outlines the female and male brain hemispheres.

ALPHA AND BETA MINDS

"The male mind thinks in terms of objects, manipulation, and power. A male mind pattern is "M" for mechanistic, A for aggressive, L for lust, and E for ego." The female mind thinks in terms of people, responsiveness and caring. A female's mind pattern could be described as "F for feeling, E for Empathy, M for meaning, A for altruistic, L for listener and E for effacing."

Sex and the Single Hemisphere: Half a Brain

Just as everything in nature exists in opposites, the cerebral cortex, or the cap on the brain where we do most of our thinking, has two opposite sides to its wholeness. Among other things, the left side specializes in verbal and listening skills, interpersonal relationships, interpretation, and finding meaning in the world. The right side specializes in doing, using, manipulating, fixing and feeling. Both genders draw from both sides in all that they do and think, but they do so in quite opposite ways.

Boys (or alpha thinkers) show earlier right-hemisphere development than girls, and this in part explains their cradle preference for things over sounds and space over people. Girls (or beta thinkers) have a more developed left hemisphere, in part explaining their general superiority in verbal skills and listening over boys' preference for doing and manipulating. Girls' brains are wired for discussion and conversation and boys' brains are set up more for doing and controlling. Because of their "testosterone poisoning", men have a built-in brain bias

71

for compartmentalized thinking, hearing and interpreting feelings less effectively, and being consumed more with carburetors than caring.

Because of their less developed corpus callosum (the part of the brain that helps our left and right hemispheres communicate with each other) boys' or alphas' brains are made to function one hemisphere at a time — what some women or betas may experience as a half-witted approach to life. They have trouble putting their right brains together with their left and their feelings together with their mouths. Their genitals seem to have a mind of their own, because the part of the brain controlling genital response is dissociated from caring, consideration, and caution. Their ability to know "why" they do what they do or the effect it has on those around them is not as developed as the female's sensitivities in these same areas.

Because women or beta thinkers have a more well-developed corpus callosum, or "brain connector," the left sides of their brains usually know and can interpret what their right brains are feeling. What a woman "does" is strongly influenced by the right hemisphere. The typical alpha thinking of the male is more segmented and feelings are more easily distanced or forgotten. The typical beta thinking of the female is more holistic and tends to blend the feelings from the right side with the facts from the left. Men sometimes have feelings about what they are doing, but women more often try to do what they are feeling.

As far back as the nineteenth century, German psychologist Gustav Fechner proposed that splitting the hemispheres of the brain would result in two separate human beings. Surgery that accomplished just this (called commissurotomy, because the commissures, or connections between the hemispheres, are severed was first done in the early 1940s as one means of controlling severe epilepsy. This surgery is still performed in rare cases today, and studies of approximately 300 patients who have undergone this treatment reveal that their left brains have no "idea" what their right brains are experiencing.

Alpha and beta thinking patterns are two opposite mind personalities that can be combined into a relationship of One mind that unifies both male and female thought styles. The alpha style is more "particular" or segmented and partialistic in its approach to life. The beta cycle is one of waves of energy and emotion."

Summary of Gender Differences:

Women seem to regard questions as a way to maintain a conversation. Men view questions as requests for information.

Women tend to connect "bridges" between what their conversational partner has just said and what it is that they have to say. Men do not generally follow this rule and often appear to ignore the preceding comment by their partner.

Women seem to interpret aggressiveness by their partner as an attack that disrupts the relationship. Men seem to view aggressiveness simply as a form of conversation.

Women are more likely to share feelings and secrets. Men like to discuss less intimate topics, such as sports and politics.

Women tend to discuss problems with one another, share their experiences, and offer reassurances. Men, on the other hand, tend to hear women (as well as other men) who discuss problems with them as making requests for solutions, rather than as simply looking for a sympathetic ear.

Deborah Tannen, P.h.D., in her book, "You just don't understand: women and men in conversation", outlines the cross cultural communication of men and women.

UNDERSTANDING A WOMAN'S LANGUAGE OF CONNECTION AND INTIMACY

Women speak and hear a language of connection and intimacy, while men speak and hear a language of status and independence. Rather than dialects; men and woman are known to speak different genderlects.

Intimacy is primary in a world of connection where individuals form networks of friendship. In the world of status, independence is primary, because a means of establishing status is to tell others what to do, and taking orders is a marker of low status. Though everyone needs both independence and intimacy, men tend to focus on the first and women on the second. These differences often give men and women different views on the same situation.

Love, oh love, oh careless love.

75

THE EARLY DEVELOPMENT
OF COMMUNICATION

It all began when we were just kids:

The claim that men and women grow up in different worlds may seem absurd. After all, brothers and sisters grow up in the same family; they are children to parents of both genders. How do men and woman learn different ways of speaking and hearing?

Even if children grow up in the same neighborhood, on the same block, or in the same house, girls and boys grow up in a world of different words. People talk to them differently and expect and accept different ways of talking from them. Children learn how to talk and how to have conversations from their parents and their peers. Boys and girls have different ways of talking to their friends. Although, boys and girls play with each other, they spend most of their time playing in same-sex groups. Although some of the activities they play are similar, their favorite games are different. Their use of language in their games are separated by a world of difference.

Boys tend to play outside, in large groups that are hierarchically structured. Their groups have a leader who tells others what to do and how to do it, and resists doing what other boys propose. It is by giving orders and making them stick that high status is negotiated. Another way boys achieve status is to take center stage by telling stories and jokes, and by challenging stories and jokes of others. Boys' games have winners and losers and elaborate systems of rules that are frequently the subjects of arguments. Boys frequently boast of their skills and argue about who is best at what.

Girls, on the other hand, play in small groups or in pairs; the center of a girl's social life is a best friend. Within the group, intimacy is key: Differentiation is measured by relative closeness. In their most frequent games, such as jump rope and hopscotch, everyone gets a turn. Many of their activities (such as playing house) do not have winners or losers. Though some girls are certainly more skilled than others, girls are expected not to boast about it, or show that they think they are better than the others. Girls don't give orders; they express their preferences as suggestions, and suggestions are likely to be accepted.

Whereas boys say, "Gimme that!" and "Get outta here!" girls say, "Let's do this," and "How about doing that?" Anything else is put down as "bossy." They don't grab center stage -- they don't want it -- so they don't challenge each other directly. And much of the time, they simply sit together and talk. Girls are not accustomed to jockeying for status in an obvious way; they are more concerned that they be liked.

These childhood development patterns shed light on the views of woman and men in relationships. The principal importance in the boys' hierarchical world is status, and the way to achieve and maintain status is to give orders and get others to follow them. A boy in a low-status position finds himself being pushed around. So boys monitor their relations for subtle shifts in status by keeping track of who's giving orders and who's taking them.

These dynamics are not the ones that drive girls' play. The principal importance in the girls' community is intimacy. Girls monitor their friendships for subtle shifts in alliance, and they seek to be friends with popular girls. Popularity is a kind of status, but it is founded on connection.

Adults learn their ways of speaking as children growing up in separate social worlds of peers. The conversation between women and men is a cross-cultural communication. Misunderstandings arise because the gender communication styles are different.

Why do men resist in seeking information; while women readily ask questions?

There are two simultaneously different messages implied in seeking and giving information. Men and women focus on two different angles. By offering information, the information itself becomes a message. The fact that one person has the information, and another person spoken to doesn't, sends a message of superiority. The one who has the information is put higher on the hierarchical ladder; and is considered more competent and knowledgeable. Men easily identify with this perspective; as a means of self-respect. Because of this men often resist in receiving information from others, especially from women. Frequently women are cautious about stating information that they know, especially to men.

Giving Help - Receiving Admiration:

The message found in giving and receiving information is also found in requests for help. Many women not only feel comfortable seeking help, but feel honor-bound to seek it, accept it, and display gratitude in exchange. Many men feel honor-bound to fulfill the request for help whether or not it is convenient for them to do so.

Our days will be
so ecstatic
Our nights will be
so exotic
For I'm a neurotic erratic
And you're an erratic erotic.

79

There is a balance between seeking help and showing appreciation. Women and men seem equally bound by the requirements of this arrangement. Women are bound to show appreciation, even though a man has not helped. A man is bound to invest time and energy that he really couldn't spare, in attempting to help.

THE INTIMATE CONNECTION

Women look to their closest relationships as havens in a hostile world. The center of a little girl's social life is her best friend. Girl's friendships are made and maintained by telling secrets. For grown women also, the essence of friendship is talk, telling each other what they are feeling and thinking. When asked who their best friends are, most women name other women they talk to regularly. When asked the same question, most men will say it's their wives. A man's second choice is usually men they occasionally play sports with or a friend they haven't spoken to in over a year.

To a man, talk is for information. So when a woman interrupts her partner when he is reading the newspaper; he assumes that she has to tell him something. To a woman, talk is for interaction. Telling stories is a way to show involvement, and listening is a way to show interest and caring. It is no coincidence that she always thinks of things to tell him when he is reading.

Understanding genderlect improves relationships. Once people realize that their partners have different conversational styles, they are inclined to accept differences without blaming themselves, their partners, or their relationships.

Understanding the others' ways of talking is a giant leap across the communication gap between men and women, and a giant step towards opening lines of communication.

Afterward:

The "Gentleman's Black Book" has undoubtedly given useful tools and information to assist men in communicating with women. But the most important element is to get out there and approach as many new ladies as your situation allows. Don't take rejection to heart; play the numbers game and most importantly don't give up on love. There is a wonderful woman somewhere out there; who is waiting to meet to you.

K. Hicks

**"CANADIAN AWARD
WINNING DESIGNERS"**

LOURO
JEWELLERS

DESIGNERS & CRAFTSMEN
OF FINE JEWELLERY

24 BELLAIR, YORKVILLE
TORONTO, ONT. MSR 2C7
(416) 961-4653